Four Men of God

STUDIES IN THIS SERIES

Available from Marshall Morgan & Scott

How to Start a Small Group Bible Study A Guide to Discussion Study

Mark: Examine the Record (recommended as first unit of study)

The Acts of the Apostles

Romans

Four Men of God Abraham, Joseph, Moses, David

FOUR MEN OF GOD
Abraham—Joseph—
Moses—David

17 Discussions for
Small Group Bible Study

Marilyn Kunz and
Catherine Schell

small group bible studies

MarshallPickering
An Imprint of HarperCollins*Publishers*

Marshall Pickering is an Imprint of
HarperCollins*Religious*
Part of HarperCollins*Publishers*
77–85 Fulham Palace Road,
Hammersmith, London W6 8JB

First published in Great Britain
in 1985 by Marshall Morgan and Scott
Reissued in 1992 by Marshall Pickering

3 5 7 9 10 8 6 4 2

Originally published in the US by
Neighborhood Bible Studies Inc.

Bible verses quoted in this guide are taken from
the *New American Standard Bible*

A catalogue record for this book
is available from the British Library

ISBN 0 551 01203 X

Set in Times

Printed in Hong Kong

Contents

How to Use
This Discussion Guide

Each study guide in the Small Group Bible Study series is prepared with the intention that the ordinary adult group will, by using this guide, be able to *rotate the leadership of the discussion*. Those who are outgoing in personality are more likely to volunteer to lead first, but within a few weeks it should be possible for almost everyone to have the privilege of directing a discussion session. Those who are new to the Bible, including those who are still investigating its claims and have not yet committed themselves to Christ, will take responsibility for asking the questions from the guide, as well as those who are familiar with the Bible or newly converted or even mature Christian believers.

Reasons for this approach are:

1. The discussion leader will prepare in greater depth than the average participant.

2. The experience of leading a study stimulates a person to be a better participant in the discussions led by others.

3. Members of the group which changes discussion leadership weekly tend to feel that the group belongs to everyone in it. It is not "Mr. or Mrs. Smith's Bible study."

4. The Christian who by reason of spiritual maturity and wider knowledge of the Bible is equipped to be a spiritual leader in the group is set free to *listen* to everyone in the group in a way that is not possible when leading the discussion. He (she) takes his regular turn in leading as it comes around, but if he leads the first study in a series, he must guard against the temptation to bring a great deal of outside knowledge and source material which would make others feel they could not possibly attempt to follow his example of leadership.

(For study methods and discussion techniques refer to the first booklet in this series, *How to Start a Small Group Bible Study,* as well as the following suggestions.)

Aims of this study series

1/ To learn to know Abraham, Joseph, Moses, and David — four men who put their trust in God.

2/ To learn more about God as he is revealed in the experiences of these men.

3/ To apply what is learned to our living today.

How to prepare a study as leader or participant

1/ Pray for wisdom and the guidance of the Holy Spirit.

2/ Using a modern translation of the Bible, read the *background passages* indicated for each study *as well as* the actual *discussion sections.* Though the passages are long, they are narrative in style, interesting in content, and can be read quickly. Then *reread* the sections for discussion. As you read:

   a/ Make a chronological outline of the character's life. Note particularly any experiences with God and with men that seem to be crucial in the man's development.

   b/ Consider the man's family background and his social position in the life of his time.

   c/ Especially observe the man's spiritual experience and the development of his relationship with God.

   d/ The Eternal God has not changed, and people have the same basic needs and many of the same problems that they did in Old Testament times. So watch for lessons that you can learn from the lives of these four men and their relationship to God.

3/ Use the discussion questions and cross references provided by each lesson in this study guide. Think through the answers as you find them in the Bible passages. Since it takes several studies to cover the life of each character, try to see one week's study in the context of the other studies on a particular man's life.

4/ If you are preparing to lead the discussion, rephrase the prepared questions in your own words and according to your own understanding. You may wish to use this sheet of your own questions as you lead the group discussion rather than the booklet.

5/ Pray for ability to guide the discussion with love and understanding.

How to lead a discussion study using this guide

1/ Begin with prayer for open minds to understand, and willing hearts to obey, the Word of the Lord. You may ask another member of the group to pray if you have asked him ahead of time.

2/ Allow five minutes or so for all to glance over the discussion passages in order to focus their thinking on the study.

   a/ It is not possible to take time to read aloud all the discussion passages so that everyone should prepare by reading them *before* he comes to the study.

   b/ If your group cannot or will not prepare ahead of time, then you will need to spend two or more sessions on each lesson in order to have time to read the discussion sections aloud together at the beginning of the session. If you do this, try to keep your aim in sight which is to study the man's character, not all the many lines of thought which arise out of the events described in these narratives.

3/ Guide the group to discover what the passage says by asking the study guide questions which you have revised and supplemented so that they have become your own.

4/ Keep in mind that this is a character study and that it will not be possible to do a careful verse-by-verse analysis of the passages in the limited time available. Your purpose is *character study*.

5/ If you are leading the second or any following study on a man's life, begin your discussion with a brief review of what has been learned about him, mentioning the previous events of his life only as they relate to your description of his character.

6/ Consider together the summary questions for the study, and encourage each member of the group to be honest in self-appraisal. You take the lead in spiritual honesty.

7/ Bring the discussion to a close at the end of the time allotted. Close the meeting using the written prayer at the end of the study for the day.

8/ *Remind the group of the background readings for the study for the next week and encourage them to begin to prepare for the study early in the week.*

How to encourage everyone to participate

1/ Encourage discussion by asking several people to contribute answers to a question. "What do the rest of you think?" or "Is there anything else which could be added?" are ways of encouraging discussion.

2/ Be flexible and skip any questions which do not fit into the discussion as it progresses. Often, in answering one question a group will go on to answer other questions before the discussion leader asks them. In that case, these questions need not be asked and the leader can proceed to the next relevant question.

3/ Deal with irrelevant issues by suggesting that the purpose of your study is to discover the *character* of the man revealed in the study passages. Suggest an informal chat about tangential or controversial issues after the regular study session is dismissed.

4/ Receive all contributions warmly. Never bluntly reject what anyone says, even if you think the answer is incorrect. Instead ask in a friendly manner, "Where did you find that?" or "Is that actually what it says?" or "What do some of the rest of you think?" Allow the group to handle problems together.

5/ Be sure you don't talk too much as the leader. Redirect those questions which are asked you. A discussion should move back and forth between members, not always coming back to the leader. The leader is to act as moderator. As members of a group get to know each other, the discussion will move more freely.

6/ Don't be afraid of pauses or silences. People need time to think about the questions and the passage. Try *never* to answer your own question. Use an alternate question if the first question seems difficult for the group to understand.

7/ Watch hesitant members for an indication by facial expression or body posture that they have something to say, and then give them an encouraging nod or speak their names.

8/ Discourage too talkative members from monopolizing the discussion by specifically directing questions to others. If necessary, speak privately to the over-talkative one about the need for discussion rather than lecture in the group and enlist his aid in encouraging all to participate.

Introduction

"And those who know thy name put their trust in thee, for thou, O LORD, hast not forsaken those who seek thee" (Psalm 9:10).

Abraham, Joseph, Moses, David — each of these men holds a strategic place in history. Abraham was the father of the people of God. Joseph was the agent of their deliverance from death by famine, Moses led them out of captivity in Egypt to the boundaries of Canaan, and David established the kingdom and ruled over Israel as God's regent. These men revealed certain qualities of character which we do well to emulate. In particular, each is noted for an attribute found in perfection in Jesus Christ: Abraham for obedient faith, Joseph for mercy toward those who betrayed him, Moses for meekness and sacrificial love for his rebellious people, and David for humility as God's anointed king.

These four men met situations of challenge and temptation which tested and developed them. In the following studies we shall consider their experiences in terms of our lives as Christians. God who led these men still seeks men and women who will obey him, who will put his glory and his purposes before their own pleasure. Through such people God will accomplish his objectives in the world today. We have the opportunity to know God, to serve him, and to be the agents of his blessing to our generation as Abraham, Joseph, Moses, and David were to theirs.

ABRAHAM — THE FRIEND OF GOD

Today people are eager to be known by the friendships they have. Men in public life like to be known as "a friend of labor" or "a friend of business" or "a friend of civil rights." We proudly announce we are a friend of a certain person or a particular family. Friendship meant a great deal in times past, also. It was because Abraham was granted the privilege of repeated experiences of personal fellowship with God that he came to be called the friend of God (James 2:23; 2 Chronicles 20:7; Isaiah 41:8). These four studies from the life of Abraham deal with God's call to him, the many consequent tests to his faith, and Abraham's failures and victories in faith. The character of God is revealed throughout in his dealings with Abraham.

ABRAHAM
An Adventurer for God

Genesis 12:1-20; 13:1-4

1. What is the Lord's initial call to Abram? What promises are included? What is Abram asked to relinquish? What impression do you get of the extent to which God intends to involve himself in Abram's life? Compare God's call to Abram to a human proposal of marriage.

2. How does Abram respond to God's call? (See also Hebrews 11:8.) At what point does the Lord appear again to Abram? When and why does Abram build the first altar? the second altar?

3. Why does Abram go to Egypt? In view of God's promises in verses 1, 7, how should Abram have reacted to the famine? (See Psalm 37:3, KJV, RSV*.)

4. Having failed to trust God for food in the land of promise, what danger and consequent temptation does Abram face in Egypt? How does Abram act in Egypt? How does God intervene to prevent further wrongdoing and, at the same time, to rebuke Abram?

5. What does Abram acknowledge by retracing his steps and returning to the altar at Bethel?

Genesis 13:5-18

6. How does Abram handle the problem which arises between his herdsmen and those of Lot? What further insight does this give you into Abram's character? What confidence must a man possess to risk or give up such material wealth for spiritual gain? Give a present-day example.

---

*KJV — King James Version of the Bible
RSV — Revised Standard Version

7. How is Abram's generosity toward Lot regarded by the Lord? What additional promises does God now make to Abram? How does Abram respond? Compare Abram's situation with the Lord Jesus' promise in Matthew 6:31-33. Which takes priority in your life — self-interest or obedience to God?

Genesis 14:1-24

8. Why does Lot get into trouble? Note 13:12, 13. How does Abram react when he learns of Lot's difficulty?

9. Describe the encounter with Melchizedek and the king of Sodom. Of what two things about God does Melchizedek remind Abram? How does this reminder prepare Abram to face the king of Sodom's tempting offer? What does Abram's response in these interviews reveal about his sense of values (verses 20b, 22-24)?

Genesis 15:1-21

10. How is the Lord's message to Abram in 15:1 appropriate in the context of the events of chapter 14? Note that Abram now has four powerful kings as enemies (14:17) and also that he has given up great material rewards (14:22, 23). In this context, see God's word to us in Hebrews 13:5, 6. What is to be our security and the object of our affections?

11. What is the reason for Abram's distress (verses 2, 3)? By way of answer, what specific promises does God give to Abram? Compare 15:5 with 13:16.

12. How does Abram respond (verse 6) to the Lord's astounding declaration? Upon what does Abram base his belief? See Romans 4:1-5, 23-25 for the implications for us of Abram's faith. Is your hope of salvation based on the holy character of God and his free gift of righteousness in Christ, or on your own works?

13. List in two columns God's few commands and his many promises to Abram (12:1-3; 13:14-17; 15:1, 4, 5, 7).

14. What covenant or pact does the Lord make with Abram (verses 7, 18-21)? What visible and acted pledge of his promise does God give to Abram (verses 9-17)? What future events are revealed to Abram (verses 13-16)? (*Note* — Here

an ancient form of contract or covenant is described in which sacrificial animals were divided into halves, and the two parties to the covenant passed between them. In this particular covenant, only a symbol representing the Lord (verse 17) passed between the pieces, indicating that God alone was undertaking the fulfillment of all the conditions of this covenant.)

SUMMARY

1. How has the Lord initiated his relationship with Abram in chapters 12-15? What do these chapters reveal about Abram's God?

2. What do chapters 12-15 reveal about the man Abram? What are his weaknesses and strengths? What spiritual qualities does he exhibit?

3. Which of Abram's qualities do you desire in your life? What actions and attitudes do Abram's failures warn you to avoid?

CONCLUSION

Abram possessed the spiritual daring to leave his home and go to a new land in response to God's call. In this new land which God had promised to him, Abram was able to hold his possessions lightly, allowing Lot the first choice of the land. Abram's greatest step of courage and of faith in this section occurs in Genesis 15:6 where he believed God for the impossible.

PRAYER

O God, who calls each of us from our former ways to live in a covenant relationship with you in a new land of spiritual reality, grant us the sensitivity to hear your call and the courage to obey and venture forth with you. We pray in Jesus' Name. Amen.

the society, which I acquired by covenant is reflected in those specific amounts once divided into before and are now just the fourth... ... between... In our political economy... ... agreements... our final... ... based between my plans, indicating that God made you one, ... having the fulfilled in accordance with the conditions of the Agreement.

SUMMARY

1. How has the Lord enabled his relationship with those in Galatians 3:1-5? What do these chapters reveal about the Mosaic Law?

2. What do chapters 6 to 15 reveal about the Holy Spirit? What are his various gifts and strengths? What spiritual significance does it involve?

3. ... which, personally, multiply, do you obtain in your life? What actions and reactions can Abram's conduct move you to avoid?

CONCLUSION

Abram possessed the spiritual strength to leave his home and go to a new land in response to God's call. To do this land when God had promised to him. Abram was tested in his obedience by being willing to let his first child be killed. Abram's greatest acts of courage and of faith made his decision to trust God is where he belonged then for the Lord's ultimate will.

PRAYER

"O God who calls each of us from our varied ways to live in a constant relationship with you in a new and deeper spiritual being, grant us the sensitivity to hear your call and the courage to obey and venture forth with you. We pray in Jesus' Name. Amen."

ABRAHAM
The Ups and Downs of Faith

Genesis 16:1-16

1. How long a time has elapsed from God's first promise of descendants to Abram (12:1-4; 16:3, 16)? What action does Sarai decide to take toward obtaining children, and why? (Sarai and Abram's action was contrary to God's intention for marriage, but permissible under the laws of their culture.)

2. Why does Sarai soon regret her action, and whom does she blame? What problems have you fostered when impatience or unbelief led to your taking things into your own hands?

3. What elements of God's character are revealed in his dealings with Hagar?

Genesis 17:1-27

4. Compare the circumstances surrounding the encounters between God and Abram in 15:1, 7, and 17:1. How does God identify himself to Abram in each case? Note in each instance that the command and/or promise follows the revelation of God about himself. Why?

5. Why is Abram's name changed? (Abram means "high father"; Abraham means "father of a multitude.") Discover each promise God makes here to Abraham. How does the Lord emphasize to Abraham that a relationship with God is basic to everything else he promises (verses 7, 9, 14)?

6. What responsibility does Abraham have (verses 9-14)? What does God choose circumcision to represent (verse 11)? (Circumcision was in use in Abraham's time as a tribal mark.) How would a visible symbol such as circumcision be of spiritual help to Abraham at this time?

7. How is Sarai involved in the promise? How do you account for Abraham's response to God in verses 17, 18 after his response to God's promise in 15:4-6? What specific things are foretold (verses 17-21)? Why is faith for the very specific promise sometimes more difficult to practice than faith for the more general promise?

8. How and when does Abraham act in response to God's promises (verses 22-27)?

9. How long has it been since Sarah and Abraham's attempt to solve the problem of an heir in their own way? What problems to faith arise because of our view of time? Why is waiting always a test to faith?

Genesis 18:1-33

10. In what new way does God appear to Abraham? How does Abraham react? Compare Sarah's reaction in 18:12 with that of Abraham in 17:17. Why does each laugh? What does each question? When are we apt to have similar reactions? How are we affected by the faith or lack of faith of those nearest to us?

11. What is the answer to the Lord's question in verse 14? Why is Sarah afraid? Why is her denial useless?

12. Why does the Lord reveal his plan concerning Sodom and Gomorrah to Abraham (verses 17, 18)? Why does Abraham intercede for Sodom? What does Abraham's intercession reveal about his understanding of the character of the Lord?

What does Abraham's intercession reveal about his own character (verses 25, 27)?

SUMMARY

1. Trace Abraham's spiritual development as revealed in chapters 16 through 18.

2. From Abraham and Sarah's experiences in chapters 16 through 18, what do you learn about faith in God — its growth, its difficulties and hindrances, its results? Give some practical examples of faith and of unbelief from your own experience.

22

CONCLUSION

There are times in a person's life when the greatest expression of courage is the willingness to wait. Although Abraham was weak enough in his faith so that he went along with Sarah's plan to obtain the descendants God had promised, he still was basically committed to God's promise and he responded in obedience to God's commands. Abraham's intercession for the righteous who might be in Sodom and Gomorrah showed his belief in the just character of God and his faith in the Lord's promise to bless the nations of the earth through Abraham.

PRAYER

Almighty God, the faithful and just One, help us to live in the light of your promises. Keep us from presumptuous thoughts and from unbelief. Help us to trust you with the impossible, and keep us from interfering. May we not neglect our responsibilities for intercession in prayer, but come to you on the behalf of others as your servant Abraham did. We pray in the name of Jesus Christ who is at your right hand interceding for us. Amen.

ABRAHAM
Facing Problems

Genesis 19:1-38

1. Describe the situation the two angels find in Sodom. Lot seems to be an important man in Sodom as indicated by the fact that he is sitting in the gate (verse 1). How much actual respect does he command there (verses 9, 14)?

2. What effect does Abraham's intercession with the Lord (18:22-33) have upon the outcome of events in Sodom (19:12-16, 29)?

3. Why does this tragedy come upon Lot (13:11-13)? What effects has Lot's decision to settle in Sodom had upon his family? (Note 19:14, 16, 24-26, 31, 32, 36.) Consider the possible long-range effects of your choice of social and business relationships upon yourself and your family. Discuss.

Genesis 20:1-18

4. Some twenty-four years after the events of 12:10-20, Abraham faces a similar temptation. What continues to be an area of weakness for Abraham? Why (verse 11)? What are your particular areas of fear and worry?

5. How does the Lord deal with Abimelech (verses 3-7, 17, 18)? What is revealed about the Lord in these dealings? What sort of person is Abimelech shown to be?

6. Note Abimelech's stinging rebuke (verses 9, 10). How does Abraham try to excuse his own actions to Abimelech? Why is half-truth or deception by omission of certain facts as destructive here as a complete lie? For God's command to us see Exodus 20:16; Ephesians 4:22-25.

Genesis 21:1-34

7. How and when is the Lord's promise to Abraham (17:

16, 19; 18:10, 14) fulfilled? How long has it been since the Lord's first call and promise to Abraham? (See 12:1-4; 21:5.)

What tests has such a length of time placed upon Abraham's faith? For what have you had to wait in faith?

8. Where does the child get his name (17:17, 19)? (*Note* — Isaac means "he laughs.") What are Sarah's reactions to Isaac's birth? Compare 18:12, 13. How must Abraham feel at Isaac's birth?

9. What is the meaning of Abraham's circumcision of Isaac (verse 4)? See 17:3-14.

10. How does the result of Abraham and Sarah's earlier lack of faith come back to trouble them? What decision does Abraham have to face? What do his reactions to Sarah's request and to God's command tell us about Abraham? (Compare 21:10-12 with 17:18, 19.)

11. How does the Lord again intervene to care for Hagar? What does this reveal about the character of God?

12. What do you learn about Abraham from the way he handles the dispute with Abimelech's servants over the well? Compare Abraham's right actions here toward Abimelech and the happy result with their previous encounter in chapter 20.

13. In the land of the Philistines, how does Abraham make public acknowledgment of his faith in the Lord? What new name for God is mentioned? (*Note* — The long-lived evergreen tamarisk tree was an excellent symbol of the unchanging character of the everlasting God.)

SUMMARY

1. Review the different types of problems faced by Abraham in chapters 19 through 21.

2. Discuss what you have learned from Abraham's life concerning what to do or what not to do when: (1) relatives or friends face disaster because of their choices and/or environment (Genesis 19); (2) fears cause us to do things which endanger or hurt others (Genesis 20); (3) difficult choices arising out of past failures must be made (21:1-21); (4) there is a dispute over rightful ownership of property (21:25-32).

CONCLUSION

Abraham faced family and business problems not so different from our own. Though the basic pattern of his life evidenced an active growing faith in the Lord, Abraham did have areas of obvious weakness and failure. Even when Abraham failed to trust him, God proved himself faithful. Abraham saw the years of waiting for his long-promised heir rewarded with the miraculous birth of Isaac to Sarah. He witnessed God's loving care and concern for all men in the deliverance of Abimelech, Hagar, and Ishmael from the evil consequences of his own weaknesses and failures.

PRAYER

Dear Lord, deliver us from those nagging, often groundless fears which paralyze us or cause us to act foolishly as Abraham did when he denied that Sarah was his wife. Forgive us for the half-truths and deceptions in which we have indulged. Grant us boldness to live in the light of reality through the power of our Lord Jesus Christ. Amen.

ABRAHAM
The Supreme Test

Genesis 22:1-19

1. To see what is included in the expression "after these things" (verse 1), review briefly Abraham's experiences of God's faithfulness up to this point (chapters 12-21).

2. What is the test the Lord gives to Abraham? How does the very phrasing of the command make it clear that God understands the cost to Abraham? Note the continual emphasis throughout this incident upon the bond between father and son (verses 2, 3, 6-10, 12, 13, 16). Sometimes we may think that God does not really understand how we feel. How does such a concept affect our reactions to God's commands in difficult circumstances?

3. In Abraham's day it was not uncommon for Canaanite fathers to sacrifice their firstborn as the highest act of worship to their gods. Imagine Abraham's conflicting emotions upon hearing the Lord's command. Throughout this incident, what sort of relationship is revealed between Abraham and Isaac? What spiritual danger does Abraham face in his great love for his son (Exodus 20:1, 3)? What does the fact that Abraham sets out early the next morning indicate as to who comes first in his heart?

4. What provisions does Abraham make, and who accompanies him? What provision does he not make? In contrast, during times past before Isaac's birth, in what ways did Abraham try to skirt difficulty or take things into his own hands?

5. How long does the test continue? What thoughts, memories, and questions must fill Abraham's mind during these days? See 17:18, 19, 21.

6. What does Isaac question as he and his father go up the mountain? Imagine Abraham's feelings at this point. What

confidence does Abraham reveal in his answer to Isaac? How has he resolved the apparent conflict between what God has promised to do through Isaac and what God now demands that Abraham shall do with Isaac (Genesis 22:2, 5, 8; Hebrews 11:17-19)?

7. What do you learn about father and son when Abraham binds Isaac and lays him on the altar?

8. How far is the test carried? Why? What has this test proved? What does it mean to "fear God" (verse 12)? In what sense does God who knows all things come to know from this test that Abraham fears him?

9. How and why is God's promise to Abraham renewed (verses 15-18)? See also Hebrews 6:13-15. How is the whole world to be affected because of Abraham's obedience?

10. What new understanding, do you think, has Abraham received from this experience as to God's will concerning human sacrifice? concerning God's faithfulness to keep his promises? concerning God's ability to provide for every need?

11. What impression must this incident and its outcome have made upon the young Isaac?

12. It has been said about the Bible that the New Testament is concealed in the Old, and the Old Testament is revealed in the New. Consider the experiences of Abraham and Isaac in this chapter as a picture of the events involved centuries later in the sacrifice of Jesus Christ, the Son of God. What parallels and what contrasts do you note? (John 1:29; 3:16; 10:17, 18; Luke 22:41-44; 23:35; Mark 15:34; 16:6)

Genesis 23:1-20

13. At Sarah's death, instead of carrying her body back to the land of his fathers for burial, how does Abraham express his faith in God's promise to give the land of Canaan to his descendants?

Genesis 24:1-9

14. What concern does Abraham have regarding a wife for Isaac? What dangers would there be in Isaac marrying a Canaanite?

15. What clear instructions does Abraham give to his servant regarding his mission (verses 4-9)? What expectation does Abraham have of God's help in this matter? What practical connection does God's sworn promise (verse 7) have with Isaac's need for a wife?

Genesis 25:1-11

16. In giving Abraham Isaac, God apparently rejuvenates Abraham's physical powers so that he becomes the father of many other children. However, what careful provision does Abraham continue to make regarding Isaac (verses 5, 6) in the light of God's promise (17:19-21)?

17. What is emphasized about Abraham in the description of his death (verses 7-11)?

SUMMARY

1. Describe the character of Abraham as it is revealed in the incidents of chapters 22-25. How does Abraham show himself to be the friend of God? Compare with John 15:14 where the Son of God states what it means to be his friend.

2. What do the events of Abraham's life reveal about the character and power of God?

3. Why does God's test in our lives come in terms of what is dearest to the heart? What or who is the object of your worship?

CONCLUSION

In the ultimate test of his faith, Abraham was asked to trust God, not with his own life, but with that which was dearer than life to him, his only son. In this test Abraham's confidence in the power and faithfulness of God had to be acted out in obedience to God's command to kill Isaac, the very embodiment of all God's promises to him. Abraham's faith rose to the test and he acted in expectation that, if necessary, God would resurrect Isaac from the dead to fulfill all that he had yet promised to do through him. This test effectively removed any danger that Isaac would occupy the place in Abraham's heart that rightly belonged to God, his Creator, Lord, and Friend.

PRAYER

O Lord of Abraham and Isaac, heavenly Father, remove from my heart all those things I have so long cherished that they seem a very part of myself. Root them out so that you can enter in and make my inmost being your dwelling place. Reign there, Lord, without a rival. Be the Light and the Love of my heart. For the sake of your Son, Jesus Christ, Amen.

JOSEPH — A MAN OF MERCY

Anxiety, tension, and strain are so common-place among us that the person who is free from them is considered unusual. These debilitating factors produce physical ailments, mental distress, and spiritual depression. In popular writings analyzing this situation, the blame for these things is often placed upon our surroundings and the pressures of modern life. In the following three studies on the life of Joseph we shall see a man who experienced all the negative circumstances necessary to destroy a person, but who triumphed over them. The secret of Joseph's development into a man of mature and godly character is open to anyone who will study his life and learn from it.

JOSEPH — A MAN OF MERCY

JOSEPH
Wronged and Tempted

Genesis 37:1-11

1. What do you learn in verses 1-4 about the location, occupation, emotional climate and relationships of Joseph and his family?

2. What reasons do you observe for Joseph's brothers' resentment toward him? How does Jacob fail to help this situation of sibling rivalry? What would you have done in Jacob's place?

3. Describe Joseph's two dreams (verses 5-11). What is their effect upon his family? What two reactions does Jacob seem to have? What does his telling of the dreams show about Joseph?

Genesis 37:12-36

4. Describe the feeling of his brothers toward Joseph. When have you had similar attitudes or observed them in others?

5. Describe briefly the chain of circumstances which lead to Joseph's being sold into slavery in Egypt.

6. What cruel deception do Joseph's brothers use against their father? How does Jacob receive the news? How must the brothers feel during Jacob's bitter mourning? Why is jealousy such a destructive emotion, even when good grounds exist for it? How can jealousy be dealt with (Colossians 3: 5, 12, 13)?

7. Imagine Joseph's feelings as he is taken to Egypt and then sold to Potiphar. What change in status does Joseph experience? What changes does he face in the emotional atmosphere of his life?

8. How do young people sometimes react when removed

from their home surroundings? How could Joseph easily have talked himself into becoming "an angry young man"?

Genesis 39:1-6a

9. Describe Potiphar and how Joseph fares in his household. What insight does Potiphar have, and what does he do about it?
10. What success and what new responsibilities come to Joseph? Why?

Genesis 39:6b-23

11. Why does Joseph refuse Potiphar's wife? What effect would her continued demands have? Why must the temptation to please her have been very strong? Why didn't Joseph yield to this temptation?
12. Why is Joseph thrown into prison? Imagine his feelings at this point. What new temptations would the very injustice of his situation bring? How does verse 21 make all the difference? In every circumstance, what awareness does Joseph seem to possess?
13. Why does Joseph have "success" even in adverse circumstances?

SUMMARY

1. What would you list as Joseph's strengths and weaknesses?
2. What circumstances could have caused Joseph to feel that God had deserted him? What events revealed that God was with him? How do you judge whether God is at work in your life?
3. What sacrifice did Joseph make to preserve his personal purity? Why? See Hebrews 12:7-11 for the reasons God commands us to resist sin.

CONCLUSION

If ever there was a man who had reason to succumb to anxiety, bitterness, disloyalty and sexual immorality, it was

Joseph. Although he was greatly wronged by his brothers and by Potiphar's wife, Joseph did not give in to vengeful thoughts or self-pity. Both Potiphar and the jailer became aware of a special quality in Joseph. He worked faithfully on the task at hand and gave loyal service when it would have been very easy to do otherwise. While God did not prevent Joseph's betrayal by his brothers or his unjust imprisonment, he did go with Joseph and bless him in the midst of these difficult situations.

PRAYER

Lord Jesus, Prince of peace, we confess that we and those about us are tempted to meet the difficult circumstances of our lives with tranquilizers or with alcohol, seeking in these the deliverance from tension and bitterness. By the vitality of your Holy Spirit, please deliver us from the self-pity, self-concern and self-centeredness which would destroy us. Help us to discern your hand in the circumstances of our lives so that we may truly entrust ourselves and our loved ones to you. Grant us spiritual victory over the cutting remark, the threatened job failure, the pressure to sin. Amen.

JOSEPH
Disappointment and Waiting

Genesis 40:1-23

1. What circumstances bring Joseph into contact with two officials from Pharaoh's household? What can you surmise about the atmosphere of the Egyptian court from this situation?

2. In spite of his own troubles, how does Joseph manifest his interest and concern for others? What is your attitude toward the problems of others when you have deep troubles of your own?

3. Why is Joseph confident that he can understand the real meaning of the dreams of these two men? Why does Joseph desire to come to Pharaoh's attention? How could the butler forget Joseph?

4. Imagine Joseph's feelings as he gradually realizes that the butler had failed to act on his behalf. What defense does the godly man have against disappointment? Why is waiting so often a factor in God's plan for deliverance? What effect does waiting have? See Psalms 25:4, 5; 40:1-3; 62:1, 2, 5-7.

Genesis 41:1-57

5. What circumstances finally lead to the Pharaoh's learning about Joseph? Why is this a far more auspicious time and way than if the butler had remembered Joseph two years earlier?

6. Compare how Pharaoh probably would have viewed Joseph two years earlier with how he views him at this point. What evidence have you had in your own life of the wisdom of God's timing?

7. What testimony does Joseph give before Pharaoh? What

does this reveal about Joseph's spiritual maturity and courage? What changes do you observe in Joseph from the boy who told his brothers about his dreams?

8. How does Joseph interpret Pharaoh's dream? What does he emphasize to Pharaoh about God (verses 16, 25, 28, 32)?

9. In verses 33-36, what recommendations does Joseph make? What reaction is there to his suggestions? What does Pharaoh recognize as the source of Joseph's wisdom? What is Pharaoh's estimate of Joseph? In consequence, what changes are made in Joseph's position and authority (verses 39-45)?

10. How has Joseph been prepared in Potiphar's service and in prison for his new responsibilities? God never wastes anything. How has he used hard times to prepare someone you know for greater service?

11. Why does Joseph name his sons Manasseh and Ephraim? How are others blessed through Joseph?

SUMMARY

1. What new temptations did Joseph face in chapters 40 and 41? Why are the sins of the spirit often more difficult to overcome than the sins of the flesh? What counsel would you have given to Joseph during this period of testing, waiting, and disappointments?

2. How was God's perfect timing revealed in Joseph's life? How did Joseph meet his great opportunities when they came?

3. What did Pharaoh learn about God from Joseph? What opportunities are available to you to give testimony about the Lord?

CONCLUSION

Sometimes things seem to go from bad to worse. If there is a faint ray of hope and that hope is crushed, the disappointment which results can lead to discouragement and even despair. Joseph's darkest moment must have come when he realized that the one man who could have helped him had either failed or forgotten about him. Waiting taught Joseph the priceless lesson that his redemption and deliverance would not come by his own wit or by the influence of another, but by the hand of God.

PRAYER

Heavenly Father, we thank you that your mercy and love can reach us even in our disappointments, our discouragement, and despair. We thank you that there is no circumstance of our lives about which you do not know. When we sit imprisoned by our fears and sorrows you are with us, ready in your time to deliver us to greater joy and peace and responsibility than we could dream of. Teach us, Lord, to wait for you. We pray in the Name of your Son who is able to help those who are tempted because he himself has suffered and has been tempted. Amen.

PRAYER

JOSEPH
Forgiveness

Genesis 42:1-38

1. Describe Joseph's two interviews with his brothers. How does seeing his brothers affect Joseph? What effects do these interviews have on Joseph's brothers?

2. Why are these brothers so disturbed when Joseph demands that they bring their youngest brother to Egypt, and later when they discover the money in their sacks? Why does sin often cause a man to regard all later distressing circumstances in the light of his own wrongdoing?

3. How do you account for Jacob's reaction to this situation (verses 36, 38)? Why is Benjamin so precious to his father? What dilemma does Jacob face?

4. What condition has Joseph given for Simeon's freedom (verses 18-20)?

Genesis 43:1-34

5. How is Jacob (Israel) persuaded to change his mind? What commands does he give, and what is his prayer?

6. How are the brothers treated when they arrive again in Egypt (verses 16-34)? What are their reactions?

7. Imagine Joseph's emotions during their meal together. What must be his thoughts?

Genesis 44:1-34

8. What, do you think, are the reasons for Joseph's plan (verses 1-5)? What rash promise do the brothers make (verse 9)? How does the steward amend their pledge (verse 10)? Why?

9. How does Joseph push his brothers even further (verses

14-17)? What appeal does Judah make? Compare with Genesis 37:25-28.

Genesis 45:1-28

10. Why would Joseph be so touched by Judah's appeal? How have Joseph's feelings been building up? (See Genesis 42:7, 23, 24; 43:30, 31.)

11. What has characterized Joseph's attitude toward his brothers from the time that they first came down to Egypt?

12. What is Joseph's understanding of all that has happened to him? Who really sent Joseph to Egypt? Why? See verses 5, 7, 8. How does Joseph describe God's blessings to him?

13. Why should an awareness of the mercy of God to us lead us to show mercy toward others? Compare Matthew 18:23-35; Ephesians 4:31 to 5:2.

14. How is Joseph's mercy manifested toward his brothers? In what specific ways can you show mercy to others?

15. Why, do you think, does Pharaoh show such generosity to Joseph's brothers? Compare Ephesians 1:6 (*The Living Bible* translation): "Now all praise to God for his wonderful kindness to us and his favor that he has poured out upon us, because we belong to his dearly loved Son."

16. How do you account for Joseph's admonition in 45:24? How can we help our children to overcome the sin of blaming others for their own failures?

SUMMARY

1. Read aloud Genesis 50:15-21. How does this paragraph summarize the attitudes of the brothers and of Joseph revealed in today's study?

2. What continues to be the basic contrast between the attitudes of Joseph and his brothers?

3. Compare Joseph's words in Genesis 50:20 with Romans 8:28. How did Joseph experience the truth expressed much later by Paul?

4. What should be the Christian's attitude toward all the circumstances of life, including the unpleasant things?

44

CONCLUSION

Joseph recognized no second causes in his life, but he acknowledged the hand of God in every circumstance. Because he was keenly aware of God's mercy to him, he showed mercy in his dealings with his brothers. How much more should every Christian show mercy to others because he has experienced the greater revelation of God's mercy in forgiveness and cleansing of all his sins through Jesus Christ!

PRAYER

Almighty Lord, God of purity and grace, in asking your forgiveness I can claim no merit of it. I cannot plead extenuating circumstances or the weakness of my sinful nature, nor can I blame the persuasiveness of others who led me astray. I can only pray, forgive me for the sake of your Son who died for me, Jesus Christ, my Lord. And because you have freely forgiven me, grant me the grace to forgive those who have sinned against me. Again I pray through Jesus Christ, our Lord. Amen.

MOSES —
LEADER AND DELIVERER

Every generation needs men of foresight and high purpose to be its leaders. "Where there is no vision, the people perish" (Proverbs 29:18, KJV). A man who fails to see spiritual realities and to seek God's purposes will fail to lead his people in the right direction. The life of Moses provides a picture of the elements essential in effective leadership. It is important to observe not only the national changes accomplished through Moses' leadership, but also the changes produced in Moses himself. God is always as concerned with the worker as he is with the work.

MOSES
Call to Leadership

Exodus 2:1-25

1. What is the situation of the Hebrews at the time of Moses' birth? As to the reasons for this, see Exodus 1:8-14, 22. How is the infant Moses rescued from death?

2. Moses' awareness of his Hebrew ancestry and his faith in the true God may well have come from the first years of his life when his own mother was his nurse. What privileges and opportunities would come to the child growing up as the son of Pharaoh's daughter? See Acts 7:21, 22.

3. Though a prince in Pharaoh's household, with whom does Moses identify himself? What concerns does Moses have? How is his attempt at leadership among his own people received? How do you account for this early rejection of Moses' leadership? For the comment of the New Testament on this incident, see Acts 7:23-29.

4. Why does Moses flee? Consider what his attempt to defend his own people has cost him. What indicates Moses' continuing attitude toward oppression and injustice (verses 17, 19)?

5. What strengths and weaknesses does Moses display in this chapter?

6. Though Moses is in exile in Midian, what is God's attitude toward the condition of the Hebrews (verses 23-25)? Note the four verbs describing God's awareness of their situation. Have you ever felt that the very opposite of verses 24, 25 is the situation in your life — that God doesn't hear, etc.?

Exodus 3:1-22; 4:1-31

7. Describe the changes in Moses' life since he fled from Egypt. To what luxuries, leisure, and cultural opportunities

has he doubtless been accustomed in Egypt? Of what would a shepherd's life consist? How would both experiences, the life of a prince and the life of a nomad shepherd, prepare Moses for the task of delivering Israel?

8. What purpose does the flaming bush serve? What does Moses learn about God in verses 2-6? How does this revelation affect Moses?

9. Note the detailed expression of God's concerns and purposes in verses 7-10. What is Moses' response? What major emphasis has Moses missed in the Lord's statements in verses 8 and 12? Compare with 2 Corinthians 3:4-6a. What is God's answer to Moses' sense of inadequacy?

10. Trace the series of responses Moses makes to God's call. (See 3:11, 13; 4:1, 10, 13.) After God answers Moses' logical questions, what personal objections does Moses raise?

11. How does God answer each of Moses' questions and objections? What promises and provisions for Moses does the Lord make? At what point, and why, does the Lord become angry with Moses?

12. What issues are involved in the task before Moses (3:18-22; 4:21-23)? What preparation does Moses have for Pharaoh's reaction? Whom will Pharaoh actually be opposing?

13. How does Israel now respond to Moses' claim to leadership? Why is their reaction so different this time? (2:23-25; 3:12; 4:29-31)

SUMMARY

1. What principles of preparation for leadership may be drawn from Moses' experiences in these chapters? Why wasn't Moses ready to deliver his people in chapter 2? What did he need to learn about himself, about others, and about the Lord? Compare Romans 12:3; Philippians 4:12, 13; 2 Corinthians 3:5.

2. Consider Hebrews 11:24-27 as an example of the cost of spiritual leadership. What value judgments did Moses make? Suggest practical examples of similar value judgments which the Lord may require us to make in our day.

3. How does the Lord regard oppression? For what reasons and to what purpose were the Israelites to be freed from their slavery in Egypt? To what purpose have you, if you are a Christian, been delivered from the bondage of sin? See 1 Peter 2:9, 15, 16.

CONCLUSION

All about us are opportunities for exercising leadership, but we need to avoid the two mistakes Moses made in regard to his call to lead his people. At first Moses thought that his awareness of the people's need for deliverance was enough, and he was self-assertive and overconfident. When the Lord did call him to leadership, Moses had swung to the opposite extreme and was paralyzed by a sense of inadequacy. When the Lord calls a man as he called Moses, he enables him for the task. God's leaders are those whose confidence is in the Lord, who follow and obey him.

PRAYER

Lord, we thank you and praise you for those whom you have called to spiritual leadership in our generation. Grant them an awareness of your presence and direction in their undertakings. Forgive us for being satisfied with things as they are, for failing to see things from the perspective of your purposes in our lives. Grant us eyes to see you, ears to hear you, and hearts to obey you, that your kingdom may come and your will be done on earth as it is in heaven. In the name of our Lord Jesus Christ who taught us so to pray. Amen.

MOSES
Challenges to His Leadership

Exodus 5:1-23; 6:1-13

1. What relationship have Moses and the reigning Pharaoh quite possibly had previously? Note Exodus 2:10, 23. Remember that Moses is no stranger to the Egyptian court.

2. Describe the encounter between Pharaoh and Moses. What moderate request does Moses make? What is Pharaoh's response?

3. How does the interview of Moses and Aaron with Pharaoh affect the lot of the people of Israel? What accusation do the Israelite officers (foremen) bring against Moses and Aaron?

4. What questions does Moses bring to the Lord? Imagine Moses' feelings at this point. Compare the reaction of the people in 5:21 with their response in 4:31.

5. What is the Lord's first answer to the distressed Moses? Why is the Lord's timing different from what Moses has expected? Instead of religious freedom and the lightening of their burdens within Egypt, what does God intend to accomplish for the Israelites by Pharaoh's rejection of Moses' request (6:1, 6-8)? What may be God's purpose in delaying the answer to your prayers in a hard situation?

6. Analyze the messages to Moses (6:2-5), to the people of Israel (6:6-8), and to Pharaoh (6:10, 11). What does God say about the past? the future? List the seven promises God makes to the children of Israel.

7. What is the people's reaction? Why?

8. What is the emphasis and meaning of the phrase repeated in verses 2, 6, 8?

9. Compare Moses' objections in 6:12, 30, and 4:10.

Upon what does Moses really seem to be depending? In what should he put his confidence? How do you evaluate your resources for any task?

Exodus 7 through 12

10. As you skim quickly through these chapters, note the increasing severity of the judgments, the continuing reaction of Pharaoh, the change in what God asks of Pharaoh (5:1-3; 8:27; 10:9, 25, 26). *Make lists of these in three parallel columns.* What is the outcome of all these events (12:33-41)?

11. Note the purposes of God's great patience in his dealings with Pharaoh (9:13-16, RSV). Compare Romans 2:4, 5; Proverbs 29:1.

Exodus 13:17-22; 14:1-31

12. Why does Pharaoh pursue the Israelites? How do the people of Israel react? What does this reaction reveal about their understanding of God's power and Moses' leadership?

13. How does Moses respond this time under the pressure from the people and the danger from Pharaoh? What does Moses urge the people to do? When you face a situation of apparently overwhelming disaster in your life, where do you turn and what do you do?

14. What attitude toward God is required to obey Moses' command to be still (14:13, 14) and the Lord's command to go forward (verse 15)?

15. Describe the activities of each of the participants in verses 21-31. Certainly God could achieve the same ends without Moses' services in this incident. Why, do you think, does the Lord thus use Moses?

16. What effects does this incident have upon the people of Israel?

SUMMARY

1. Analyze Moses' behavior under pressure in these chapters. What, would you say, is his chief problem? About what does he express doubts?

2. What is Pharaoh's problem? In what does he put confidence? Why does he refuse to submit to the Lord?

3. What doubts and fears do the people of Israel express? Compare their fears with Moses' fears. What is the difference? What are the common fears of mankind today? of Christians?

CONCLUSION

God's twofold purpose in delivering Israel was to reveal himself to Egypt and to Israel as the one true God, almighty and worthy of their obedient worship. The release of Israel was not primarily for the purpose of political freedom but for the purpose of their worship and obedient service to the Lord. God chose to work through Moses who had to face the unbelief of his own people and the constant rejection of Pharaoh. God does not always work out the details of deliverance in just the way we expect. It is a test of our faith in God to continue in confident obedience to him in spite of all opposing powers and circumstances.

PRAYER

Almighty God, we confess that we are easily impressed by the threats and the power of the Pharaohs of our time. Forgive us that in our doubts and fears we act as if you are less powerful than an earthly ruler. Make us people of faith. Arm us with spiritual power. Help us to teach our children that you are the Creator and Sustainer of the universe, so that they may have no fear except a reverent awe of you. We pray in the Name of Jesus, the Author and Finisher of our faith. Amen.

MOSES
Frustrations of Leadership

In preparation for this study, read the full text of Exodus, chapters 15 through 17.

Exodus 15:22-27

1. What is the children of Israel's first experience in the wilderness after their deliverance from the armies of Pharaoh? What does their reaction indicate about these people? Why is it so difficult for us to remember the Lord's former deliverance in each new situation?

2. What does Moses do when the people murmur? According to verses 25b, 26, what is God's purpose in allowing this situation?

3. What does the Lord require of his people and what promise does he make? What does the Lord want the people to realize about him?

4. What is God's purpose in allowing us to face disappointment and trial? See 1 Peter 1:6, 7; James 1:2-4.

Exodus 16:1-12

5. Of what do the people of Israel accuse Moses and Aaron? Why? What do they recall about Egypt? What have they apparently forgotten (Exodus 1:13, 14, 22)? How must Moses feel?

6. How is one's faith tried under circumstances of physical discomfort? Why do we, like the people of Israel, tend to make poor value choices in such instances?

7. What is God's provision (verses 4, 5, 10-12)? What is the Lord's purpose in making this sort of provision for his people's need?

8. How do Moses and Aaron interpret the situation? What do they want the people to realize about their deliverance from Egypt? about their murmurings? about the Lord?

9. Describe an experience you have had when people murmured and complained about something. What effect does such an atmosphere of discontent have? Why is complaining inappropriate for a Christian (Matthew 6:30-34; 1 Thessalonians 5:16-18)?

Exodus 17:1-16

10. What happens to put Moses under new pressure? What indicates the extent of the people's discontent with Moses' leadership?

11. Note that Moses continually warns the people of the spiritual nature of their complaints and demands (16:8; 17:2). How are they maligning the character of God as well as that of Moses?

12. How does verse 7 identify the real issue at stake?

13. What contrast do you observe between Moses and the people throughout these incidents? Moses suffers the same physical problems that they do. Why are his reactions different?

14. Give a practical example of how we as Christians can emulate Moses rather than the people of Israel.

15. Imagine the emotions experienced by the people of Israel, so newly released from an oppressive enervating slavery, when they are attacked by new enemies. How has Israel's experience at Rephidim prepared them to meet the attack of the Amalekites?

16. Describe the battle which takes place between Israel and Amalek. What, do you think, are God's purposes in this battle? Whose participation is required for Israel's victory (verses 9-13)?

17. What have you ever done to help in a situation like that described in verse 12? (*Note* — The uplifted hands symbolized the heart uplifted in intercessory prayer, thus teaching the value of prayer and man's complete dependence upon God alone. By upholding Moses' body, Aaron and Hur also

strengthened his mind and spirit for the work of prayer.)
What is the responsibility in spiritual battle of those who take
offices in a church? What would have happened if Aaron and
Hur had been negligent?

SUMMARY

1. Make a list of at least five or six things that you think
Moses learned from the experiences outlined in these passages.

2. Why didn't Moses just turn around and take the people
back to Egypt when they complained? What special temptations must the events of these chapters have brought to
Moses?

3. Considering the lessons of this chapter, what advice
would you give to a young pastor who is discouraged by the
criticisms of his congregation?

CONCLUSION

Moses experienced the frustrations of leading a complaining
people. Their bad attitude increased his burdens of leadership and their own misery. For Moses these were experiences
of learning the limitations of human leadership, and of realiz-
ing his own dependency upon the Lord. He also learned the
value of faithful companions through the help he received
from Aaron and Hur.

PRAYER

Good Shepherd, we remember your promise that you came
that we might have life and have it abundantly. Daily we receive your mercy and provision, yet we are a complaining
people living in the midst of plenty. Forgive us that we com-
plain about being overweight when so many suffer real hun-
ger. Forgive us that we are a wasteful, destructive people.
Forgive us for being quick to criticize others and slow to
recognize the same faults in ourselves. Deliver us from the
murmuring spirit which infects us and destroys those who live
with us. In your Name we pray, Lord Jesus. Amen.

MOSES
The Cost of Leadership

In preparation for this study, read the full text of Exodus, chapters 32 through 34.

Exodus 32:1-14

1. How do you account for the actions of the people and Aaron in verses 1-6? See Exodus 24 (especially verses 12-18) for the circumstances of Moses' departure and how long he has been gone. Compare the people's actions (32:1, 4-6) with what they have very recently committed themselves to obey (20:2-4; 24:3).

2. Compare verse 4, verse 7, and verse 11. In each case, who is given credit for delivering the people from Egypt? by whom? The people's rejection of the Lord leads to his rejection of them as his people.

3. What judgment does the Lord intend to bring upon the people (verses 9, 10)? What great opportunity does he offer Moses? Consider the attractiveness of this offer to Moses. How is God's offer a test of Moses' character?

4. What is Moses' plea? Upon what does he base his plea (verses 12, 13)? What does this incident reveal about Moses? What qualities of mature leadership does he exhibit?

Exodus 32:15-35

5. What does Moses do when he returns to the camp of Israel? Compare Aaron's testimony (verses 23, 24) with verses 3, 4.

6. How does Moses seek to redeem the situation in verses 25-29? (Those slain would be those still persisting in the idolatrous orgies in spite of Moses' return to camp and his ac-

tion in verse 20.) What indicates that Moses is not vindictive toward the people (verse 30)?

7. Describe Moses' intercession and the result of it. State briefly what the terrible events of chapter 32 have cost Moses. What are the consequences of the people's rebellion against the Lord? Suggest an illustration of how a Christian parent or a Christian leader might experience a similar situation and such opportunity for intercession.

8. Consider Moses' behavior throughout this chapter as an example of the responsibilities and the cost of mature leadership. How does Moses feel about sin? about his people? about the Lord?

Exodus 33:1-11

9. What further consequence of the people's rebellion against the Lord is revealed? How do the people react to God's refusal to go with them?

10. What do verses 7-11 reveal about the pattern of Moses' spiritual life? Why is spiritual leadership ineffectual without such habits of regular communion with God? What effect does Moses' habit of communion with God have on other people (verses 7, 10)?

Exodus 33:12-23

11. What three major requests does Moses make of God (verses 13, 15, 18)? How are his prayers answered? What do verses 15, 16 indicate about Moses' evaluation of his task to take the people into the promised land?

12. Why do people sometimes confuse work for the Lord with his presence? What tragedies result?

13. Given a choice of succeeding (entering the promised land) without God or failing (remaining in the wilderness) with God, what decision does Moses make? Why may we sometime have to make a similar decision?

14. What does this section reveal about the Lord? Consider, for example, the Lord's relations with the people, with Moses; the Lord's attitude toward his promises.

15. Describe Moses' second encounter with the Lord on Mount Sinai. What qualities in the nature of God are emphasized? How does Moses respond and what plea does he make?

16. What is God's part of the covenant in verses 10-11a? the people's part? Why is obedience always the essential element in man's part of a covenant with God?

SUMMARY

1. In these chapters Moses is faced with the greatest test of his leadership. What is it? How does he meet it? Describe the nature of Moses' intercession.

2. What are the areas in which you have responsibility for intercession for others before God?

CONCLUSION

Moses refused the opportunity to desert his rebellious, difficult people and to go on alone with God. Moses also refused the temptation to think that he could go on with the people without the presence of the Lord. Moses could not live a private life alone with God, free from responsibilities to other men, nor could he live a life of political power without the strength which came through his fellowship with the Lord. Moses' way of life is summed up in Exodus 33:15, "If thy presence will not go with me, do not carry us up from here." Moses would go nowhere, even to the completion of his God-given journey to Canaan, without an assurance of God's presence with him.

PRAYER

Heavenly Father, we praise you for the intercessory work of our Lord Jesus Christ on our behalf. We give thanks that he knows our every weakness and fear, and that he has promised always to be with us. We commit ourselves in faith to him. Give us new insight into the needs and problems of others for whom we ought to pray, knowing that you desire to express your loving concern for them through our prayers. Amen.

MOSES
Leadership Tested

Numbers 11:1-35

1. It has been more than a year since Moses led the people out of Egypt (Numbers 10:11-13, 33). What is the recurring attitude of the people (11:1, 4-6)? In view of Moses' intercession for the people in verse 2, what must be his feelings when they ask for meat? How do you feel if you are with people who are ungrateful and constantly complaining?

2. What does Moses' prayer in verses 11-15 reveal about his own mood at this point? What two needs does he express (verses 13, 14)?

3. How does the Lord answer both parts of Moses' prayer? According to verse 23, what is Moses' real need?

4. When Eldad and Medad prophesy in the camp, Moses' servant Joshua is concerned lest this evidence of God's working in other people detract from his master's position as the leader of Israel. How does Moses respond (verse 29)? What happens to the leader whose chief concern is his own reputation and power? What is Moses' concern?

Numbers 12:1-16

5. What added burden is placed upon Moses by those who should be his most loyal supporters? What is the real reason for Aaron's and Miriam's opposition to Moses (verse 2b)?

6. What characteristic of Moses is brought out by the fact that he does not try to defend himself against Aaron's and Miriam's attacks upon him? Define this quality (verse 3). Compare Proverbs 16:32; Matthew 5:5. (*Note* — William Barclay describes the meek man as one who has his passions, instincts, and impulses under discipline, who is "so God-con-

65

trolled that he is always angry at the right time, but never angry at the wrong time.")

7. "If I'm meek, won't people walk all over me?" How is this question answered by the events of verses 2c, 4-16? What reason does the Lord give as to why Aaron and Miriam should have been afraid to speak against Moses?

8. How does Moses react to Miriam's punishment? What does this reveal about Moses? Why, do you think, is Aaron not stricken? How is Moses' intercessory prayer answered? How is the whole camp affected by Miriam's sin?

Numbers 13:1-3, 16-33

9. What are Moses' instructions to the twelve men sent to spy out the land of Canaan? On their return, what do they report? What is the recommendation of the majority of the spies? Of the minority?

Numbers 14:1-45

10. Describe the reactions of the people of Israel (verses 1-4) to the spies' report and to their differing recommendations.

11. How do Moses and Aaron, Joshua and Caleb respond to the people's declared intentions (verses 5-9)? What brings these four men to an opposite conclusion from that of the people when all of them look at the same situation in Canaan?

12. Compare verses 11-19 with Exodus 32:7-14. What tremendous offer of personal glory does Moses refuse in both instances?

13. In the previous incident Moses argued that the Egyptians would think that God had evil intentions in bringing the Israelites out of Egypt and Moses asked God to remember his promises to Abraham, Isaac, and Israel (Jacob) to multiply their descendants and to give them the land of Canaan as a permanent possession.

What reasons does Moses give now in asking for pardon for the people? Note how Moses pleads on the basis of the added revelation of God's character given to him after the previous incident (verse 18 is a quotation of Exodus 34:6, 7).

14. How is God's judgment mixed with mercy in answer to Moses' intercession for the people? Compare verse 12 (God's original intention) with verses 20-38. List the specific things God says will happen, and the reasons.

15. What is the continuing difference between the people and Moses in their response to the Lord's word (verses 39-45)?

SUMMARY

1. List the qualities of God's character revealed in his dealings with Moses and with the people of Israel in the incidents of today's study.

2. For what particular quality of character was Moses noted (Numbers 12:3)? How did he show this quality in the passages studied today?

3. What other qualities in Moses are revealed in the situation created by the Israelites' refusal to trust the Lord and to go on into the promised land?

CONCLUSION

The greatness of Moses is revealed in many ways in this study. When the burden of leadership became too heavy for Moses, God put his Spirit upon seventy elders of Israel to aid Moses in governing the people. Unlike many great men who are not great enough to relinquish power to necessary helpers, Moses gladly accepted these leaders and rejoiced that God's Spirit was upon them.

When Miriam and Aaron spoke in envy against him, Moses did not retaliate and he interceded for Miriam when God punished her with leprosy. Moses' refusal to seek position and glory for himself left God free to defend him far more effectively than Moses could have done.

Even when the people of Israel refused to enter the promised land to which God had been leading them out of slavery in Egypt, Moses did not reject them when God offered him the opportunity. Moses' intercession prevented their immediate destruction and he accepted with them the sentence of forty years' wandering in the wilderness.

PRAYER

O Lord God, I am so easily upset and oppressed by the complaints, shortsightedness, and unbelief of those around me. Grant me the strong grace of true meekness as it is shown in the life of your servant Moses. Work within me the humility and faithfulness of the Lord Jesus, who suffered for me. Grant to me your faithful love for my family, my friends, and my neighbors, that you may be free to use me in my situation as you were free to use Moses in his. For Jesus' sake, I pray. Amen.

MOSES
Leadership Tested, Handed On

Numbers 20:1-13

1. Though the date of this event (verse 1) is not certain, many take it to refer to the beginning of the fortieth year of wandering in the wilderness. How do the people express their complaint against Moses and Aaron? Note especially verses 4, 5. With the added sorrow of the recent death of Miriam, imagine how Moses must feel at this point.

2. What is the Lord's command to Moses (verse 8)? How does Moses fail to obey (verses 9-11)?

3. How does God evaluate Moses' action (verses 12, 24)? Why is the judgment upon Moses so severe? How has Moses failed God? Compare with the sin of the people at the time the spies reported on the promised land (Numbers 14:11). For Moses' response to God's judgment, see Deuteronomy 3:23-29.

Deuteronomy 31:1-22

4. What does Moses emphasize in his final instructions to Israel (verses 3-6)? Why might the people be afraid to go on without Moses? Why don't they need to fear?

5. What do verses 7, 8 reveal about Moses? Why do some men find it difficult to retire gracefully, to give over leadership to another? How must this incident affect the people? How must it affect Joshua?

6. What careful preparations does Moses make for the preservation of the law in future years (verses 9-13)? What does Moses believe to be essential for the people of Israel in the new land?

7. What does the Lord reveal to Moses about the future (verses 16-18)? What preparation for this does the Lord com-

mand? What is the purpose of Moses' song? How do we see the power of songs today to affect thoughts and actions?

Deuteronomy 32:1-47

In the centuries following Moses' death, this song would be a reminder to Israel of the character and power of God who had brought them out of Egyptian slavery and had given them their own land.

8. How does Moses contrast the unchanging faithfulness of the Lord with the anticipated unfaithfulness and perversity of Israel (verses 1-18)?

9. What terrible judgments of God upon Israel (verses 19-34) and upon Israel's enemies (verses 35-43) are predicted?

10. What is Moses' clear command to the people after he has recited this song to them? What reasons does he give (verses 44-47)?

Deuteronomy 32:48-52; 34:1-12

11. What is God's final command to Moses? What are God's reasons for not allowing Moses to lead the people into the land of Canaan? In Deuteronomy 3:25, Moses requested to "go over" and "see the good land." How does God temper his judgment on Moses with mercy (32:49, 52; 34:1-4)?

12. Describe Moses' death. What indicates that Moses' death was not due simply to old age (34:5-7)?

13. What was unique about the relationship between Moses and the Lord? How is Moses compared to the prophets who followed him (34:10-12)?

SUMMARY

1. For what particular quality of character was Moses noted (Numbers 12:3)? Yet, in one incident, Moses failed in what had previously been his strongest point of character (Numbers 20:10-13). How was this incident a failure in meekness? Note Psalm 106:32, 33.

2. Why is one's strongest point of character sometimes the

very place at which his greatest failure may come? Give an example.

3. Summarize briefly Moses' qualities as a man, and as a leader.

CONCLUSION

Moses' long life may be divided into three periods of forty years each — a prince in Egypt, a shepherd exile in the wilderness, and the leader of Israel. His preparation for the leadership of Israel included the finest education of the Egyptian court, the practical experience of desert living, and long periods of communion with God. Moses' faith and patience were sorely tried by his people — that large company of former slaves who were easily frightened, fickle, complaining, and rebellious. Bearing the burden of responsibility for Israel's physical and spiritual welfare, Moses is revealed as a man of humility and meekness, great wisdom, and strong faith in God, a man who cared more for God's honor than for his own glory.

PRAYER

O LORD, who spoke with Moses face to face, who delivered Israel from Egypt and preserved them through the wilderness, who proved faithful when your people failed you again and again, deliver us from a complaining, ungrateful, bitter spirit. Make us like your faithful servant Moses in loving obedience, in meekness and humility. In the name of Jesus Christ, your Son, who was faithful in everything he did. Amen.

DAVID — A MAN AFTER GOD'S OWN HEART

In recent years the civilized world has seen the rapid spread of an attitude of rebellion against authority. Already many countries face a rising tide of social problems resulting from this attitude. David was a man whose recognition of the authority of God affected the way he won a kingdom, how he ruled it, and how he preserved it. As God's servant and the shepherd of God's people Israel, David is known as a man after God's own heart (1 Samuel 13:14).

"He chose David his servant, and took him from the sheep-folds; from tending the ewes that had young he brought him to be the shepherd of Jacob his people, of Israel his inheritance. With upright heart he tended them, and guided them with skilful hand" (Psalm 78:70-72, RSV).

DAVID
Success and Exile

In preparation of this study read the full text of 1 Samuel, chapters 16 through 22.

1 Samuel 16:1-13

1. Describe the scene in which David is anointed by Samuel. What does the Lord want Samuel to learn from this experience? Why doesn't God simply tell Samuel from the outset that David is the chosen one?

2. What does this incident reveal about David and his family? What change takes place in David at this anointing?

1 Samuel 17:1-58; 18:1-30

3. Why does David go to the battlefield? What situation does he discover there? What reaction do the men of Israel have to Goliath's challenge? What reward is offered to any man who kills Goliath?

4. How does David's view of the situation (verse 26) differ from that of the other Israelites? What is Eliab's response to David? How does Saul react when David volunteers?

5. What gives David confidence (verses 34-37)? What truth has he learned from past experiences? What present opportunities do you have to trust God so that you may be prepared to face greater emergencies in days ahead?

6. What protection does David refuse? Why? What does David recognize as his real security? See also Psalm 118:6, 8, 9.

7. How does David meet Goliath's threats and mocking? What does David believe that his victory will reveal? Restate verse 47 in modern terms. What does David recognize about himself? about the Lord?

8. How do Saul and Jonathan react to David? How do you account for the differences in their reactions? What begins Saul's jealousy of David? What would David's popularity mean politically to Jonathan as well?

9. What is happening to Saul? Why does he fear David (1 Samuel 15:26; 18:8, 9, 15, 17, 28, 29)? What various actions (verses 10-25) does Saul take because of his fear and jealousy?

1 Samuel 19:1-18

10. What plot does Saul make (verse 1)? What moves does Jonathan make to protect David? Note Jonathan's wise reasoning as he seeks to reconcile the king and David.

11. What occasions a renewal of Saul's hatred? What can one do about jealousy which keeps cropping up in his heart (Colossians 3:2, 3, 12, 13)?

12. By what means does David escape Saul's plot against his life in verses 11-18?

1 Samuel 21:10-15; 22:1, 2

13. Why is David afraid of the king of Gath? What does he do to protect himself from further assaults against his life? How does his ruse succeed?

14. What types of people gather around David? Why are these men drawn to David? Compare with Matthew 9:10-13. How would the experience of leading these men prepare David to rule the kingdom? What sympathies would he learn?

SUMMARY

1. From these chapters, what sort of person do you find David to be? In what particular areas do you think his strength lies?

2. Describe the feelings you have had in circumstances similar to the experiences of David described in these chapters: a dangerous emergency; sudden success and popularity; someone's irrational jealousy of you; rejection, exile, or being an outcast of some sort. What temptations are peculiar to each

of these situations? How does the Lord help at such times (Psalms 27:1, 5; 40:1-3; 46:1-3; 103:1-6, 15-18)?

CONCLUSION

While still in his youth David rose swiftly from obscurity to great fame in Israel, but because of King Saul's jealousy he soon found himself a hunted exile in danger of his life. This swift reversal of fortunes must have given David good cause to wonder about the meaning of his anointing by Samuel. David's faith in God and his desire to see the Lord's people victorious had enabled him to face Goliath, and even under the pressure of Saul's jealousy it is noted that "David behaved himself wisely in all his ways, and the Lord was with him" (1 Samuel 18:14, KJV).

PRAYER

O Lord God, cleanse our hearts from petty jealousies and overweening ambition for ourselves and our loved ones. Help us to walk in the simplicity of a faith that learns to trust you and desires to please you through all the changing circumstances of our lives. Grant, we pray, that we may find contentment not in position, popularity, or success, but in the awareness of your love for us in our Lord Jesus Christ. Amen.

DAVID
The Fugitive

In preparation for this study, read the full text of 1 Samuel, chapters 23 through 30.

1 Samuel 24:1-22

1. Although Saul pursues David with three thousand men, what opportunity does David have to destroy him? What is the most important thing about Saul to David? How does David protect the king? What does this incident reveal about David?

2. How may young people today learn to have a similar respect for authority? What is the basis of proper respect for authority? See Romans 13:1, 2.

3. Of what does David try to persuade Saul? What arguments does he use? For what does David pray?

4. How is Saul affected by David's arguments? What confession does Saul make? What does he foresee? What promise does Saul get David to make?

5. Describe some people today who react according to either the attitude exhibited here by Saul or by David. Why is David so generous and why is Saul so small? How do you act when an opportunity for revenge is given to you? How does David meet this test? How does this incident help to fit David to lead the nation?

1 Samuel 25:1-44

6. Why does David expect favorable treatment from Nabal? Describe Nabal. What are his reactions to David's request?

7. What is David's reaction to Nabal's refusal? What does this indicate as to the kinds of reactions of which David is

capable? What does it further reveal about his reaction to Saul in 24:6, 7?

8. What do verses 14-17 show about David and his men? What kind of person is Abigail? Why would she keep her actions (verses 18, 19) from her husband?

9. What reasons does Abigail give David to persuade him to forego his plan (verses 24-31)? What does she foresee for David?

10. Why does David give thanks to the Lord and to Abigail? How does David evaluate what has happened? Why is it wrong to avenge ourselves, even when we have been wronged (Romans 12:19, 21; James 1:19, 20)?

11. Suggest ways in which wives and mothers in particular may have opportunities to play the part of Abigail, dissuading people from violence. What do you learn of how to do this from Abigail's appeal?

12. What causes Nabal's death (verses 36-38)? What does David conclude about Nabal's death? What sort of influence, do you think, would a woman like Abigail have on David as his wife?

1 Samuel 26:1-25; 27:1

13. Why does Saul begin to pursue David again? What tactical mistake does Saul make?

14. How does David react to Abishai's tempting offer? What reasons does David give (verses 9-11)? What standard controls your ambitions for yourself and for your children?

15. In talking to Saul, what two possibilities does David suggest for Saul's enmity toward him (verse 19)? How does Saul respond to David's argument? What does Saul admit?

16. In spite of all Saul's claims and confessions, what does David now realize about him (27:1)? When does a person's word cease to be dependable? To what degree can others trust your word?

SUMMARY

1. How do you account for the apparently contradictory ways in which David reacted in the three incidents in today's

study? Why was he ready to attack Nabal, but hesitant to harm Saul?

2. What evidence of David's humility do you see in these chapters? What ruled his decisions? Why was David's restraint at his second opportunity to kill Saul even more admirable than at the first occasion? What does the Lord Jesus teach about forgiveness in Matthew 18:21-35?

CONCLUSION

David rejected the temptation to kill King Saul and take the kingdom which God had promised would be his. He was patient in the face of Saul's continued provocation. David's patience was grounded in his understanding of the righteousness and faithfulness of God. He trusted the Lord to work out the circumstances of his future, to give him the kingdom at his appointed time.

PRAYER

Heavenly Father, help us, like your servant David, to trust you in good times and bad. Keep us from taking matters into our own hands when we should wait for your deliverance. Grant us the courage to believe that your will is perfect, that your truth will prevail. Forgive us that we so quickly forget the lessons of the past. Help us to forgive others as freely as you have forgiven us in Jesus Christ. Amen.

DAVID
The King

As background for this study, read the full text of 1 Samuel 31, and 2 Samuel, chapters 1 through 12. For the transition from Saul to David's rule, see 1 Samuel 31:1, 2, 6; 2 Samuel 3:1; 5:1-5.

2 Samuel 7:1-29

1. What kind of relationship exists between David and Nathan, according to verses 1-3? When peace comes, to what do David's thoughts turn? What ideas and plans occupy your thoughts during leisure hours?

2. When the Lord reveals his plans to Nathan, how do they differ from David's plan which Nathan has approved? Of what does the Lord remind David through Nathan concerning his dwelling-place in Israel in times past? concerning his past dealings with David? In verses 5, 8 God calls David "my servant" and "prince over my people Israel." What meaning do these titles convey?

3. What wonderful promises does the Lord make to David concerning: the people of Israel? David himself? David's immediate successor? the house of God? David's line?

4. To what, do you think, do verses 13, 16 refer? See Luke 1:31-33; Mark 11:7-10.

5. How does David respond to this message from the Lord? In what ways may a person react when God says "no"? In David's prayer, what are the specific items of praise? of petition? On what does David base these petitions?

6. What would David's recollection of God's faithfulness to Israel in the past (verses 21-24) do for his confidence in God's actions in the future? What does his prayer reveal about David's attitudes toward God?

7. When we find it difficult to accept a change in the plans we have conceived from a desire to serve the Lord, what does this reveal about our motives? What can we learn from David about how to respond when God's plans involve a total change in our own plans?

8. David wanted to build a house for God. God said "no," but promised that David's son would build it, and that God would build David a house and kingdom which would be established forever. As you look at what David asked and what God answered, which was the greater privilege to have?

2 Samuel 11:1-27; 12:1-14

9. How does David happen to get involved with Bathsheba? Compare verse 1 and verse 11. Where should David have been? When are you tempted to neglect your responsibilities?

10. What action does David take, even after learning who Bathsheba is? What must be David's feelings when he gets the message in verse 5? What fears would arise?

11. What action does David proceed to take and why? Why does David's plan fail?

12. What thoughts must cross David's mind when Uriah says what he does in verse 11? How does David compare with Uriah throughout this incident?

13. What new attempt does David make in verses 12, 13 to escape responsibility for his adultery? Compare David's action with the warning and promise in 1 John 1:8, 9.

14. What is the final act of David's spiritual decline? What is it costing David as a person and as the king to murder Uriah? Suggest a similar pattern of actions that a person today might find himself following in trying to cover up a sin.

15. Note the ways in which man and God view the same act of sin (verse 27). David seems to have gotten away with it, apparently forgetting all about God.

16. What is David's reaction to the story Nathan tells him (12:1-6)? Does David see any connection between this story and his own situation? Why is this stern attitude toward the sin of others frequently characteristic of a transgressor?

17. When Nathan directly accuses David, of what things does

he specifically remind him? How does God view what David has done (verse 9)? What will be the results of David's sin (verses 10-14)? Why can't the results of sin be controlled by the sinner?

18. How does David react to the words of the Lord through Nathan? What does David understand about the nature of his sin? Compare David's frank admission of his guilt with Saul's response to Samuel in 1 Samuel 15:17-21. When you are faced with the fact of your own sin in a specific situation, what do you do about it?

SUMMARY

1. Contrast the two major incidents in this study. What does each emphasize about David spiritually? How can a man guilty of the acts described in the second incident be called a man after God's own heart?

2. Read Psalm 51:1-17. What does David do when the full impact of his sin dawns upon him? What then becomes his chief concern? Why?

CONCLUSION

At the height of his success David fell into a network of sin which continued to have ramifications for the rest of his life. "Therefore let any one who thinks that he stands take heed lest he fall" (1 Corinthians 10:12). The true greatness of David was not that he never sinned, but that he came to see his sin from God's point of view as a sin against God, a rebellion against his holiness and his righteous purposes. In Psalm 51 David acknowledged the terrible danger which sin is to a man — unrepented of, it cuts him off from fellowship with God who is the very source of life. David had acknowledged himself physically weak before Goliath and dependent upon the Lord for victory over the giant. Now he knew himself to be weak in every area of life, dependent upon God for all victories — moral, spiritual, and physical.

PRAYER

O God and Father of our Lord Jesus Christ, we humbly confess that we are not immune to the sins of the flesh, the sins of the mind, or the sins of the spirit. Have mercy on us we pray. We have accepted your gifts but have used them selfishly, carelessly, and even rebelliously. We have indulged our bodily appetites, allowed our minds to follow impure imaginations, failed to heed your word and your will. Cleanse us and forgive us for Jesus' sake. Amen.

DAVID
Sorrow Multiplied

As background for this study, read all the text of 2 Samuel, chapters 12 through 24.

2 Samuel 12:10-25

1. Review Nathan's predictions of the consequences of David's sin (verses 10-14).

2. Note the first fulfillment of Nathan's predictions. Why are the servants so fearful when the child dies? How does David explain his own behavior at the death of the child? (What hope does he have before the baby dies? What confidence afterward?) Why does the Christian have an even surer hope at such times (1 Corinthians 15:20-22, 56, 57)?

3. How is the Lord's mercy revealed in verses 24, 25? How would the birth of Solomon and God's message at his birth comfort David?

2 Samuel 15:7-18

4. What further prediction made by Nathan in 12:10-12 is fulfilled here? What would make this rebellion especially painful to David? Why are the troubles inflicted upon us by family and loved ones so much more bitter than those from outsiders (Psalm 41:9)? What recourse does the Christian have at such times? See Hebrews 13:5c, 6; 1 Peter 5:6, 7.

2 Samuel 16:5-15, 20-22

5. What added humiliation comes upon David as he flees from the rebellion of Absalom? Why does he prevent his men from killing Shimei? What does this indicate about David's understanding of God's rule in the circumstances of his life?

Compare Romans 8:28. How do you view the difficult, even tragic, things which happen in your life?

6. How does Absalom's action (verses 21, 22) further fulfill Nathan's prediction of the consequences of David's sin? What influence would David's act of adultery with Bathsheba have had upon his son Absalom?

2 Samuel 18:1-15, 31-33

7. What do verses 1-5 reveal about David's leadership and his expectation of victory? How do David's men feel about him? What does verse 5 tell about David as a father? (See Psalm 3 for David's comment on this time of trouble.)

8. How does Joab disobey David's order? For what reasons, do you think? What has Absalom done to David? (See 15: 6, 13, 14; 16:20-22.) Yet, what are David's emotions at Absalom's death (verses 31-33)? How have Nathan's predictions (12:10-12) been further fulfilled?

2 Samuel 23:13-17

9. What does this incident reveal about David's relationship with his men? What value does David place on the water from Bethlehem's well? Whom does David recognize as the only one worthy of such a gift?

10. Compare yourself with David's chief men (verses 13-17). How do you rate as the follower of a far greater Leader than David, our Lord Jesus Christ? What have you dared for the Lord?

2 Samuel 24:1, 10, 15-25

11. What sense of responsibility does David exhibit in his prayer (verses 10, 17)? What characteristics of true leadership does his prayer reveal? What would an analysis of your prayers show about you?

12. What offer does Araunah make? Why does David refuse it? What does David realize about the meaning of sacrifice to God (verse 24)? How do many of us in the church today exhibit the opposite concept of service to God? What does this

reveal about our concept of God? about our concept of our relationship to him? Note 2 Chronicles 3:1 for the later use of this site.

SUMMARY

1. How do these four studies on the life of David confirm the words of Samuel that David would be a man after the Lord's own heart? What evidences are there of David's spiritual sensitivity, and that he valued what God values?

2. What was the basic commitment of David's life to which he always returned? How did this basic commitment of David's life affect his actions as:

a youth fighting against Goliath?

a fugitive from the king's jealous wrath?

a powerful monarch with a kingdom at peace?

a sinner against man and God, when faced with his crimes?

a king facing the terrible consequences of his own sin in his family and kingdom?

CONCLUSION

When David acknowledged his sin he prayed for forgiveness, for a clean heart, and the renewal of a right spirit within (Psalm 51). "What was the answer to this prayer? First, the death of Bathsheba's child; next, the discovery of hateful crimes in his household; finally the revolt of the beloved Absalom. These — answers to a prayer for forgiveness? Yes, if forgiveness means what David took it to mean, having truth in the inward parts, knowing wisdom secretly. . . . To have his people's heart stolen from him, to have his child for his enemy, to be deserted by his counsellors and his wives, to lose his kingdom, to be mocked and cursed — this was rough discipline surely. But he had desired it; he had said deliberately, 'Make me a clean heart, and renew a right spirit within me.' . . . Adversity is in itself as little gracious as prosperity. Moral death may be the fruit of one as much as of the other. It was otherwise with David, not because adversity had any special influence over him which it has not over us, but because he accepted it as God's punishment and medicine, because he believed that God would do the good for him which adversity could not do."*

PRAYER

Father of steadfast love and mercy, we pray for ourselves and for all who this day experience the distress of sorrows. Give us the humility of David. Lift downcast eyes to a renewed vision of yourself. Cleanse hearts infected by sin and rebellion. Strengthen weak knees to move forward once more. Loosen hands paralyzed by fear or self-pity to function in your service. Infuse our spirits with your Holy Spirit that we may truly know you, whom to know is life eternal. In Jesus' Name we pray. Amen.

---

*Maurice, Frederick D. *The Prophets and Kings of the Old Testament,* pp. 63-65. Boston: Walker, Wise and Company, 1860.